LARRY GOSSELIN, OFM

Hidden Sweetness

ILLUSTRATED BY
STEVE KALAR

Hidden Sweetness
Larry Gosselin, OFM

Cover and Inside Illustrations: Steve Kalar
Cover and book design: Tau Publishing Design Department

For information regarding permission, write to:
Tau Publishing, LLC
Attention: Permissions Dept.
4727 North 12th Street
Phoenix, AZ 85014

ISBN 978-1-61956-117-5

First Edition March 2013
10 9 8 7 6 5 4 3 2 1

Published and printed in the United States of America by Tau Publishing, LLC
For additional inspirational books visit us at TauPublishing.com

TauPublishing.com
Words of Inspiration

Praise for *Hidden Sweetness*

The adventure at the core of this book is the search for the voice of love. Father Larry isn't searching for love— it clearly lies all around him. He's looking for the words and images to make that love a presence in our lives. And the fact that he succeeds so often and so well, makes these wonderful poems more than poems.

Robert Inchausti,
author of The Ignorant Perfection of Ordinary People,
Subversive Orthodoxy, *and* Thinking Through Thomas Merton *(forthcoming)*

Fr. Larry Gosselin's poetry and Steve Kalar's art are a beautiful marriage. The gentle words in these pages feed the "thirst for holiness" about which Gosselin writes with such a tender heart.

Paula D'Arcy, author of Gift of the Red Bird *and* Waking Up To This Day

---

Two issues distinguish this book in a very strong way: the poems deeply reflect the Franciscan spirituality in which Fr. Gosselin has lived his life while the voices of both Francis and Clare co-whisper with him in many of his poems. Secondly, there is a deep sense of encouragement which characterizes Fr. Gosselin's entire life and ministry, and in his poems one cannot help but find encouragement and strength. Over many years and after many profound experiences of life, Fr. Gosselin has taken time to express his reaction to life in poetry. He has generously shared his insights in this book of "Hidden Sweetness." For four years I was one of his theology teachers, and it is a joy to hear in these poems how deeply Fr. Gosselin has intertwined theology and spirituality.

Fr. Kenan B. Osborne, OFM

Words drawn toward new reverberations; Gospel episodes re-envisioned through new eyes; the love at the world's core given a new voice: these riches await the reader of Fr. Larry's *Hidden Sweetness*. Like the "Sacred Space" in the poem of that title, this book is "a place that tenders consolation."

Peggy Rosenthal
author of The Poets' Jesus *and* Praying through Poetry

Prose and abstraction can never lead you near the Great Mysteries. Only poetry, art, and beauty can speak to the body, soul, and spirit at the same time. Well, here is a truly wonderful example of poetry, art, and beauty—all in one lovely book—and experience!

Richard Rohr, OFM
Center for Action and Contemplation
Albuquerque, New Mexico

Father Larry has tasted "the hidden sweetness", and it is inexpressible. But he shows us where to find it. It is all around us, where we are, in the here and now, in the simple and in the sublime---in stars and stones and streams, in storms and sunlight. Wherever we are, in what happens in our lives, God speaks personally to us, and we know the hidden sweetness of His nearness and love. This is a very Franciscan book! Thank you, Father Larry, for your guidance."

The Poor Clares of Santa Barbara

Dear friend and brother, Pat
How does one say,
"Thank You"
properly to you, for so very much?

Dedicated to St. Lawrence, Deacon and Martyr,
and to all the "Lorenzos" of the world.

Like a great song
it is too much to try to express
inexpressible words of true gratitude.
Here is spoken a soft word of appreciation,
for you, as a "hidden sweetness" residing within.
When we speak together, or alone,
what we say becomes the earth
in which we live on.
Thank you
for affirming
my life as words
spoken to the earth.

. Larry, ofm

An Acknowledgement

I wish to graciously thank the people who have helped bring this book to fruition. You are as much a part of this as you are a part of me. I want to give my sincerest thanks to Miki Landseadel, without whose peacefulness, encouragement, and editing skill, this book would have remained a wishful dream. My deepest appreciation goes to Steve Kalar whose friendship and artistic talent is pure beauty and joy. I am deeply grateful to Jeffrey Campbell and TAU Publishing Company for accepting this work and giving me the opportunity to share my passion in printed form. I thank Linda Reize for her faithfulness and savoring the word that is proclaimed. To Ginnie and Herb Kunse, I want to express my love and appreciation for their dear friendship and ongoing supportiveness. Moreover, I am always grateful for my Franciscan family for their inspiration of life and fraternity. And at the same time, I want to thank my own family for their precious love and support over the years. Finally, I thank you the readers for allowing me this privilege of sharing a little **Hidden Sweetness** with you.

Father Larry Gosselin, OFM

A Message From the Editor

In the following pages, you will find many "altar poems' in the prayers and meditations of a Franciscan priest who has become a household name among parishioners of the Central California Coast. Known for his joyful spirit and tender care for everyone who encounters him, Father Larry Gosselin, OFM, opens the hearts and minds of fellow seekers with his inspired literary voice. Generally presented as meditative breaks before his homilies, Father's poetry is a signature element of his regular masses. Over the years those who have attended his services have requested copies of his poetry and homilies, and now, by special permission, they're available to everyone. It has been an honor to have been selected to edit Father's poems of **Hidden Sweetness**.

Steve Kalar is not only a noted California artist but a member of a very elite cadre of artists of The Dante Society. Professional accolades place him among the finest artists in the world. Moreover, his charitable efforts in the North County region of San Luis Obispo County have made significant strides in helping to advance art programs for area youth. Between the vision of Father Larry's poetry and the music of Steve Kalar's illustrations, the insights of **Hidden Sweetness** should bring warmth to your heart.

Miki Landseadel-Sanders
San Miguel, CA
March 2013

Te Adoramos Santisimo Senior Jesu Cristo

I come before you, Lord, thus filled with peace and gratitude; in joy and expectation, I look forward to what lies ahead, and to what will be revealed. There is a trusted confidence that you have given me through the test of time and life experiences. I am so very grateful to be here in this place of grace. Your goodness as the God of Mercy and Faithfulness has brought me "home to myself". I pray for the grace to continue to recreate myself in your love. May my heart be continually transformed with faithfulness to find fulfillment in your love.

Fr. Larry Gosselin, OFM

Taste the **Hidden Sweetness**
that lies within your Heart

"Taste the hidden sweetness that lies within your heart,
which God has kept for those whose lives are tender within
Place your mind in the softness of life's eternal flow.
Place your soul in the brilliance of heaven's glow;
and love Him totally who gave Himself for your love,
and you will hold Him who holds all things in truth."
–St. Clare of Assisi

Born Chiara di Favarone in 1194, St. Clare of Assisi was of noble descent. The name given her, Clare, means "bright clear light." At eleven years of age Clare saw this young man, Francis, preaching in the Piazza del Comune. Her heart was transformed by what she'd heard. Francis' words, simple and unadorned, bathed her in pure light. She was inflamed in the light of Christ and sought to "mirror" this to others through a life given to poverty and prayer. This it was proclaimed at her canonization in 1255: ***The life of Blessed Clare shines with wonderful clarity…Her life here on earth shone, after her death it illumined; on earth she radiated, and in heaven she glows. Her brilliant light, hidden in the secret cloister, radiated to the outside; from her enclosure she illumined the wide world.*** (Pope Alexander IV)

Imagine Assisi in springtime, when the poppies flame the land and air in brilliant red. This is the city where a great love began: Francis and Clare. So great was their love for God that they themselves are seasons of every soul.

May these written words illumine your soul and senses to **"Taste the hidden sweetness that lies within your heart"**.

Father Larry Gosselin, OFM

愛

Ai (Love)

"An Immense Ocean"

Words fell
like dandelion petals
in the wind.

Contents

Ai

Standing atop this pinnacle: Chimney Rock,
like an ancient great cathedral; proclaiming,
pure enchantment above this Chama valley.
Ghost Ranch, New Mexico, a sense of place.
Christ in the Desert
Yellow cliffs
Roomy skies
Strong winds
Fresh spirits
Opened hearts.
O, so precious, one is held
all alone where there is only love:
a palette on the canvas of the soul.
Precious holy one, you are formed as
earthened clay in the hands of a potter.
Created as you are, to be love, and to be
atop this mountain as light, where you are:
Here, let there be light, and let there be love,
As a clear portal, bright, pure, love and light.
Taste the sweetness hidden for those who love.

To the Sound of Grace

Awakened to the rhythm of gently falling grace
Descending anew, again upon us,
The early morning rain comes down
From the darkness, held at bay by dawn
And calms the soul.
I am led to lead
From the source of grace.
Thus the storm of fear is released
To the harbor of tranquility
And possibilities.
Today, a new day,
Seems filled with fresh nourishment.
Earth budding forth
Life renewed
By the green grass of adorned hillsides.
There the possibility lies!
Life, new and fresh with wonder.
Lord,
Help me remember
That you are coming
To a land, a people
Beset by desert.
Help me to remember
That You are always new,
And that we are made new in You.

Confident Trust

The presence of Love
Abides in childlike wonder,
Friend.
To hold the hand in warmth of One
Who rests at your side along still waters,
Gently as they flow in the current that passes.
Come into this place of welcome, you belong.
Know that you are here to be loved.
In these arms time is still.
You are held.
So, to be
Love.

Desire to Thirst

Awaken from a dream state,
Filled with desire to grasp more.
The thirst for holiness grows in me,
Where the step to reach greater heights
Plays like a cool song intoned heart-like slow.
O what power has awakened me from slumber?
The infant Jesus sleeps as a gentle flame;
His sheer warmth suns my heart aglow.
Living child, your fiery love burns
Flames beyond memory,
A force that welds.
I must confess:
I love You

Stillness of Light Becoming Tree of Life
Christmas Prayer for Peace

In
language
that only light
could know

Word came in silence. By the watches of night,
in the stillness of waiting,
A Holy Child was born to us

so that we might come to light. Came in darkness; born at night,
Transforming—to be Child, born to be light,
in the world—filled with brightness, eternal light.

You are given—to night—to day—tomorrow—and forever You are born—
in a stable crèche of a humble place in a darkened time.

Leaping dim in dusty earthen shadows, fell glorious beams of some distant star
pointing to show where we long to belong. Come let us enter!

O little space of light, so all might see rightly. Here, in this place, God became
poor so that we could be whole.

Now there is something of us in You
Becoming You in us.

Most becoming!
Coming to light.

Be coming! To light!'
Transforming—to Be…

But, tonight, Little Child, don't you cry!

As a darkened world stirred with stillness this night,
In You *even our darkness* is Radiant in Your sight.

Standing Midstream on the Mighty Columbia

Outstretched arms raised in gratitude,
Buoyant freedom.
So it seems.
On this
River of Life, Rio de Vida!
Hidden
Mystery veiled,
Reaching to the heart.
Midstream and ankle deep on this covered sandbar
The Mighty Columbia rolls on by.
So it seems.
On this
River of Life, Rio de Vida!
Ocean barges cross this trajectory path,
A passing that seemed tremulous at intervals.
That man is walking on water!
Stares pass, as we pass.
Is there recognition?
Salute this passage
Illusions of apparitions
Wonder, I wonder, holds us close.
So it seems
On this
River of Life, Rio de Vida!
One friend, Greg, a golden youth, has just passed,
Now left our side, walks on.
To begin his journey home,
He passed by this way,
"Pasa Por Aqui"
So it seems.
On this

River of Life, Rio de Vida!
Bidden
These passages
Standing midstream.
Illusions of a visionary traveler.
We pass by, as you pass on.
Walk on, as if on water.
So it seems.
On this
River of Life, Rio de Vida!
Forgotten not.
Salute His passage.
For He walked on water.
May He now carry you home.
While we walk on,
As if on water.
So it seems,
On this
River of Life, Rio de Vida!

**Soli Deo Gloria
Glory to God Alone!**

August 28, 2007
In memory of Greg Campbell
October 5, 1951-August 22, 2007

Yellow Finches Together

I saw yellow finches, singing,
bathing in the humble pond—
fluttering joy of being, cleansed together.
Water splashing asunder
Flippant joy-making
Together, lifting hearts to refresh each other—
Pure lovemaking grace.
We enter Heaven through grace,
a grace we know inside the heart.
Pure hearts cleansed in love
standing together, we know
we are not alone.
Yes, the yellow finches came to the pond today
to be cleansed together.
Their joy overcame me.

The Hunger

The real hunger begins
When the stomach is emptied.
At rest from the need to fill itself,
The heart yearns for greater awareness
Of the need for the soul to be fed with sacred food.

Food for the Soul
In emptiness is full,
In rest is passionate.
Lord, You are food.

Come reside in this place of hunger.
Come rest in the awareness of want.
Come give the soul Your good food.
Come, Bread of Life that is Alive.

Feed your people with want for food.
Feed the hungry with food of Heaven.
Feed the soul that is longing for You.

Yet Another Vineyard Grows

I've seen a vineyard with no particular address.
It grows as vineyards grow and as many people grow.
It still needs purpose and care.
Growth without purpose is growth without truth.
I see as many ways to flourish as to perish.
Take, for example, the pine trees.
They have a recipe within for constant renewal.
Then observe the desert grass.
It resurfaces each year despite endless obstacles.
What a miracle to grow!
Oh, if I could venture the question,
I would ask
"Have you ever been enchanted by the potential adventure of growing your
own life?
And if not, what would do it for you?
Just like the vineyard needs some careful tending to produce fruit,
why not step out into the fresh morning sometime, and just look around.
Do you hear yourself saying,
'The house is falling down!'
Or
'Life is a wondrous adventure!'
The grass is still growing…
The grass is still growing…
And so am I."

(an adaptation on *Evidence*, by Mary Oliver)

The Music They Heard

The song of the oriole began
as a small echo, crescendoing,
calling forth all creation to new life.
As if, summoning a symphony for the stars.
Its joyful voice came announcing springtime.
But, in the midst of winter, its triumphal song
appeared unbefitting, incongruous, prophetic,
and yet without thought
it sang its song of hope.
St. Augustine of Hippo would say,
"It is like entering a king's palace."
St. Francis of Assisi could imagine
a humble crèche on an obscure Italian hillside.
But this night it was the oriole proclaiming it.
Standing alone, among, beneath the stars,
in the woodland,
was to be alive,
to be a child again.
Some things are backwards,
children wanting to be older;
older, wanting to be a child again.
This was the night of ageless innocence.
All hearts were young in this glorious singing.
Old darkness could not restrain the youthful newborn light.
It was the child, Jesus, an infant here in our midst, born to us.
God coming, to be with us,
Us coming to be with God.
The night sang its own song
The hymn that was glorious.
Come Shepherds!
Come Wise Ones!
He comes to You!
Come to Him!
Child to child!

The Awaited Vineyard

I was tired.
I felt like sleeping in the sun.

And from somewhere, a quiet voice,
Yet a command
Seemed to say
"Come!"
"Get up. Go into the field and work."

But, it was late, the day almost spent.
The call came again, and I began to hope.
Was there still room for me?
Was I still needed?

The invitation to come to the vineyard
was generous, compelling.
Yet, what could I do at such a late hour?

Entering the field,
I heard the sound of raking.
It dispelled my cowardice.
It gave me courage.
Failure—unaccountable failure—it seemed
did not matter here.

Not failure, but distance
and refusal.
Yet, in my exhausted unworthiness,
a new awareness.

The vineyard called,
a place of inexpressible acceptance.
I awoke to generosity
unimaginable kindness
lovingly poured out
unasked for.

Such immense goodness flows like a river
Even now, even here, even with me.
So long ago, it had been forgotten.
And now, it is here.

16

Bread from Heaven

Bread, broken, shared.
Food for the journey.
Scattered among many.
Given, taken to the hungry.
As honey in a nomad's mouth,
Sweetness flows in the desert soul.
Flicking sanctuary lamp remains,
Presides in our midst, reminding.
"Those who eat this bread will live forever."
Transformed,
Taken into hands opened to receive
The promise
The nourishment
Fulfilled.
We have been food.
Broken and one,
We are the bread.
We are the hungry, still, yet fed,
Sent as bread scattered upon the water,
Bringing to life "a House of Bread"
Made from the One
Born to be shared.
The Body of Christ.

Epiphany
What the Star Said

Before your eyes were opened,
I blazed my light for centuries
Breathing my first and final word
"Come and See."
The desire to seek and find
Fills the everlasting journey of the soul.
My desire to be found by you happened when you came to
me.
Now, in your flesh,
My Star shines anew.
As you sift along the path that you follow,
Search for the spark that re-ignites all destinies.
True magi dare to enter the deep descent into the unknown
And go deeper.
Digging inward they remove all glitter and gloss,
Passing through the deserts of layered masks and myths
Following a star.
They kneel.
Offer their gifts.
And there the child is found.

Have you ever tried to wake up before the world was awake?

Have you ever arisen before the world was awake and tried to listen?
Why is it that we hear questions in our inner morning voice?

Is this world merely a rehearsal for entertainment purposes?

Is there something missing yet to come?

Who has opened the door who has not yet reached for the latch?

Who can travel the miles who has not put one foot in front of the other?

Who can behold the inner chamber who has not observed the outer castle?

Ah, you are awake, now, yet there is still plenty to see!

Quickly, then, get up from your sleep.
Put on your coat; go out into the world.
Put one foot onto fresh grass and welcome life's mystery.
Sit for a while among the weeds.
Let the wind rustle the enigma in your mind,
For the soul is, after all, merely a window,
An opening to the world, no more difficult than waking from sleep.
What was that
Which hasn't ended yet?
Something seems to be saying, "It's full, but not yet!"
Then, there is still time—
And it is still early—
And you are awake!

Anniversary Poem:

The Place I Want to Go to Again, for the First Time

How much do you want? Was asked.

How much were you given?

I answered,

"The Lord is my Shepherd, there is nothing I shall want."

Yes, but in the household of the Lord you have been entrusted,

With a talent to be returned.

You must be bold and unafraid.

A sweetened voice says, "It is God's and not yours."

There must be a longing for virtue for virtue to be.

Come to this place that is given, and earned.

I asked,

"Have I been to the place before, or am I here again for the first time?"

And so I prayed.

"Lord, bring me to the place where

I may do something useful and unpretentious."

And moreover,

"Simple, and to be used

Let me be like a flower

Or like a sparrow

Or something

To be returned,

Showing what I have earned."

Was it earned or learned?

Was asked.

If you want to talk about all this,

Come to the place where I live.

It is a house named ***Gratitude***.

A Certain Day

A certain day there came a presence to me,
a holy longing.
It confronted me.
And before it I stood,
descending into myself.
Was a choice to be made?
Or a promise kept?
Standing in the middle had ceased:
a decision forthcoming.
Was it to be "yes" or "no"?
What I heard myself saying was "I can!"
"Yes, I can and will."
I will,
To do
Your will.
With the "Yes"
came a renaming,
as a sword descending gently on my shoulder
granting honor to my task.
I walked into the field,
bravely,
free
for what lay ahead.

A Wedding Veil that Veils All Peoples

The banquet begins…again,
its lavish food prepared
and choice wine set on the table
People have gathered
Celebrating a wedding feast for love.
How did I come to be invited here?
Uncertain.
How did each one of us come to be invited guests?
Some come from a state of delight
others with scars of damage.
They bring
Hesitations,
Questions
Choices of directions
That were made.
And still we come.
How many times have you been here?
The First?
Many?
Still it feels new.
Put on a wedding garment.
Leave behind the old and take on the new.
A celebrated love, fresh life of living
My friend, you are here,
That is all that matters.
You are here!
Thank you for coming.
Take the lavish food, drink the choice wine.
Now the banquet can begin.

A Sacred Space

It is not just time, in all, but a place
that tenders consolation. Just pause
in this sacred space, so as
to entertain a presence,
in the company of angels,
with healing in their arms.
For, God, even in darkness,
radiates and remediates here.
Accustomed to the sprawl of presence,
Growing among the orchards full
of lemons, oranges, avocados,
to be so near the ocean
whose very name
gives peace,
"Pacifico"

"A people in darkness have seen a great light",
which shines above the orchards and ocean.
Everything will grow.
Everyone will be healed.
God mends the wounds for all.

Empty Water

Sitting over the words
of dutiful prescriptions—"do's and don'ts"—
as if standing in a pool of empty water,
there came a kind of whispering sigh,
like a night wind in a sea of darkness.
Memory fell like a silent echo
of everything that has ever been spoken,
announcing the true elements
that have created it all.
All torrential rains fall from heaven.
Waves of knowing wash over the empty pond.
With the night falling we begin saying, "Thank you!"
We are standing by the water, thanking it,
for we have been washed clean
in the waters of freedom to live and love.

Man in the Well

It was quite ordinary that day that I went to the well.
Actually, I was feeling quite unordinarily well about myself.
So the impulse struck me,
I would meander awhile and get to the well late.
By that time everyone would have disappeared back into their homes.
The afternoon sun was scorching, radiating a prevailing heat
that seemed to penetrate my soul.
Beads of sweat rolled from my brow.
Then I noticed him sitting alone beside the cool water.
I thought, "Who must he be, sitting there by himself?"
My first impression was, "He must be a lot like me."
Maybe he is equally shamefaced.
Getting closer, I noticed he was a dreaded foreigner.
So, very contemptuously, I approached him.
Arrogantly, I was going to ask if he needed a drink of water.
It was then I sensed something, like a particular kindness surrounding him.
His eyes caught mine;
It was at that moment
I felt as if a cool refreshment of the well had opened up, inside me.
The depth of his eyes penetrated the depth of my heart.
He then said, "It is living water for which you thirst."
That it was in Him and in me,
It was my thirst and His thirst for me.
I can't really remember all that He said to me.
It was more about how he suggested a change in the usual order.
Yes, it was that day that I came to the well.
My bucket was empty, and had been for a very long time.
But I left filled
For He showed me, myself,
Something of Himself.
And I became a river of life
Pouring out into the desert.

The Love

Some days
the sun seems to go down like a fist.
We may think
nothing can be seen of Heaven.
But it is on these days
we need to get our eyes checked
—or better yet, our diminished spirits—
The heavens have no fist.
Their arms remain open in love.
Let us then continue to hear
   —little by little—
those voices that speak to us of possibilities
  for love, for peace.
Keep listening
It's never too late!
Even when the sun seems to sink over the horizon
It might be then that we see that fist open
With an invitation to love,
More,
Even more.

The Job of Morning/Mourning
(or The Joy of Job)

Awakening early, awaiting
  the light of day came.
Night had fallen away,
  having traveled a long way.
As the days before,
 so many others have also gone.

As a child, I came upon a bridge
 that rose over torrential white water.
Over it I passed.
Through time and grace I have learned the lesson,
  that between the river and the morning light,
  there is a passage above sure evils.

It may be hazardous to know the way,
  but the path is a gentle friend.

Today, morning is still, clear and still,
  as the mission bell rings across the valley.
I pray the hour once more, over again,
  paying attention to what time has taught.
That it may be time,
  which has shown me.

To see the One who is always there,
  to know again, and to be.
In the same place I have found
  The One, who comes.
To a child awakening to a new day.

The Captain of My Soul

Walking along the lakeside, I look for you;
Beside me, I feel you are near;
Taking my hand you led me to the waterside;
There the boat waits for us to set out.

Willingly, I untie the ropes of moorage..
Again, you reassure me;
You are here in the boat;
Together we become more of what I am in you.

I must let go, and go.

Leaving my nets for fishing upon the shore,
We set out into deep waters;
For in the web of my soul
Something can be found, can be caught
Beneath the waters.

For there lies the hidden wonder: You!
With the silence of the sea,
  and the shifting of the tides,
You bid me lower the net here to take in,
That which is to be caught.
You fill me, my net; it is brimming over to the breaking point.

It is too much
  or am I too little to hold it?
It is you, Jesus, that has been given to me.
Create in me a vessel that can contain
  The abundance of what lies with you.

As I journey with you upon these waters of Baptism,
I have found the captain of my soul.

The Breadth of Affection
(Rule #13: "Don't put people in boxes")

"To wake at dawn and give thanks for another day of loving."
The Bell that wakes and makes us.

There is this spark in each person,
An ember that lies at rest,
So mysteriously alive,
That can set to fire
A hope or an aim
Of being welded:
Two are now one.
Certainly, we are asleep, until it happens.
And then caught upon a whisper of the heart,
Something forgotten or something remembered
Reminds us of who we are, and who we are to become.
Seeing a kind of distant light in the face of another
At that moment it all becomes a wonderful beginning.
Long into these days resides the burning hearth,
Tempered by passing seasons of winter and spring.
Glowing, burns a quiet, shining, lasting affection.
Cold days cannot disturb the real warmth of night.
We have talked about each other long enough to know
What are our memories, who we are, what we are to become.
And still the spark glows in these embers of love and affection,
Burns a fiery yearning in the veins for a world to be called into.
The walls of the house may be old, but we think of them as newly known.
Together at last we will be joined into the fires of eternal love that set us aglow,
Eternally.

"No longer a slave, but a child"

Paul to the Galatians

The long awaited journey has come to completion;
 there is a blessing on the wide road ahead.
Someone's trying to reach out towards its Mother.
It is a blessing of a woman following,
  until and unless she is with me and reaches me,
He cannot speak His words,
For there is a flow through her of Him.
She is hurrying and He is making good time.
In His breath is His Word.
His word is assuring, and an adoption.
You are a child, born to be
Set to freedom.
Before this, you were held in chains.
Now you are free, to be,
 to be, in my blessing, to be my very blessing.
Before the stars and the mountains,
You were destined and she was yours.
Now the light of day
Hears the bird unfurling a new song.
Generations upon generations have heard it,
But today it is new again—
"You are no longer a slave, but a child"
"You are mine. I have called you by name."
"I love you."
For I am Mother, and you are child to me.

Night Knowing

The night sky
  hides the knowing
  from that which lies hidden:
The dark night of sense and soul.
In the hiddenness there is only the sound of a cricket.
Cricket lives among the unlit ground.
  In the roots that call out.
Living reassurance
  that even in darkness there is life,
Revealing the blind lightning
   blazing the path ahead.
A kind friend,
   a voice in the darkness.
A trusted step lies ahead,
One to take in faith.
Step out,
   Step into the darkness.
You are saved.
For the One who is The Light
  Is there.

Los Ojos de los Pobres
(The eyes of the poor)

Herding sheep,
Creatures consigned to defenseless frailty,
All the more easy to snatch away, alone,
For wandering they lay prey.
But the Shepherd knows, surveys his flock,
Stands guard, over,
Having eyes for them alone.
The eyes of the sheep keep their gaze upon Him,
In Him, they see;
They move, they have their being,
For knowing He is there,
Hearing His voice reassures safety.

The eyes of the Poor,
have a light that sees,
The Good Shepherd
as He looks after them.
His eyes radiating
gentle protection over their lives.

As a poor woman cradles her infant granddaughter,
Their eyes gaze to the One whom they know
is holding them in everlasting arms.
These are the eyes that see
The Good Shepherd.

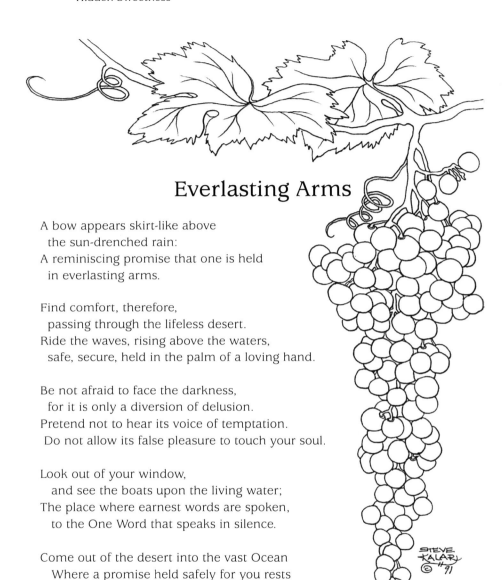

Everlasting Arms

A bow appears skirt-like above
  the sun-drenched rain:
A reminiscing promise that one is held
  in everlasting arms.

Find comfort, therefore,
  passing through the lifeless desert.
Ride the waves, rising above the waters,
  safe, secure, held in the palm of a loving hand.

Be not afraid to face the darkness,
  for it is only a diversion of delusion.
Pretend not to hear its voice of temptation.
  Do not allow its false pleasure to touch your soul.

Look out of your window,
  and see the boats upon the living water;
The place where earnest words are spoken,
  to the One Word that speaks in silence.

Come out of the desert into the vast Ocean
  Where a promise held safely for you rests
In Everlasting Arms.

Authority Resides Within

The authority of the heights
  is not the law of the valleys.
They are just not the same.
But there is a blessing between the two
  when and where they meet.
The voice that dwells from without
  belongs to a hand reaching out for the threshold.

While the knowing that comes from within
  reveals the call of years and strives to listen,
The words belonging to the soul
  hides in adornment of light within light.
It holds authority of a small place within,
  where dying, a Son has risen.

Yes, the rising of the sun,
  hides the stars of light before daybreak.
The sun first casts its morning rays upon the mountaintops,
  then reaches the valley below.
People will be waking
  to see the fresh new day
Timely revealing their enlightenment
  when the heights and valleys meet.

Atop the Summit

Atop the summit the Word came to us.
As witnesses looking on
Blinded,
Light was transcendent
Fearful,
Love was transfigured,
Infinitely,
Humanity was transformed.
Wondering, we stood in silent awe,
Alone with the Alone.
Who is this person whom we know and look upon again
As if for the first time?
We have walked in the dust with Him along the road.
And now, only now, do we know more, for
"This is my beloved Son" we heard said.
Can it be that the dove flies beyond our knowing?
We knew as we were leaving
That there is a destiny given in love,
Which seemed as if it never changes,
Though all was changing.
To have seen Him so radiant, so glorious as man,
Now with us,
among us,
walking the long road to Galilee.
Who is this man, and who am I with Him?
Blinded
Atop the summit we stood,
Transfixed,
Below the mountain, we walked,
In silent awe.

Annunciation

Spirit comes
Come Spirit!

Mother calls out a Womb
Womb calls out a Mother

Announces

A place of dwelling
To place a dwelling

Beginning a new fulfillment
Fulfillment, a new beginning

Blossoming infinitude
Infinitude blossoming

This house in Nazareth
To this house of David

Come

Unsandaled feet consecrate handmaid
Isn't this the carpenter's wife, Mary?

Divine Mystery, create the Mother of my Lord.
Fashion and soothe the prophet's call within me.

Make the greenwood from the dry
Both of us, the three of us,
Are conceived in love
Today.

A New Testament Night

Last night I had a dream;
  My father came to me.
He appeared as a little child, a boy of six,
innocent and fresh.
We stood on the ocean shore.
There, calm waves approached.
I knelt down to embrace him,
  when he spoke.
He said that this was his chance to tell me,
"Much has happened over the years,
  many journeys
  in the world and in yourself.
But, along the way,
You must know
The truth of what you believe.
Know that God is Love.
Believe only that."
He smiled at me,
  with a look of pure grace,
Words washing through me
  as waves broke over me.
He looked as if it were my chance to speak.
But I, content in silence,
Knew his words were complete.

Mere (Mirror) Honesty

The whole of creation speaks to us of transparent honesty.
The birds, flowers and trees are only what they are—
No more, no less—and they are beautiful in themselves.
A bird does not try to be anything else but itself,
And in being itself it can fly.
A flower does not try to be anything else but itself,
And in being itself it can bloom.
A tree does not try to be anything else but itself,
And in being itself it can tower.
And so we try to be ourselves,
And in doing so we can fly, we can bloom, we can tower.
This is in my mind and I know my heart is made for it.
Just as the soil belongs to the earth, so our lives and hearts must meet.

Yearning Righteousness

a season for joy
awaiting
for those who hunger
righteousness
as great saints of old
seeking such love
can tell a story
of their own
marvels worked
in them
for the holy sought
as grace
in the open heart
once again
the yearning
calls forth
to be
holy

Love

(The Gratitude)
A rendition borrowed from the style of George Herbert

Love bade me come, but my soul drew back, afraid
For standing outside I was covered with dust and sin.
But love being quick-eyed saw me growing slack
      fearing to enter into the feast.
Drawing near me, Love sweetly questioned if I lacked anything.

I answered, "Yes, I am a guest unworthy to be here."
But Love said, "You shall be here for you shall be love!"
But I questioned, "I, the unkind and ungrateful one?"
"Ah, my dear one", Love said, "I cannot look upon you, except upon you as love."
Love then took my hand, and smiling at me, I replied with sorrow in my eyes.

Seeing my tear's response, Love said, "Who made your eyes but I?"
"True," I answered.
"But, you see, I have marred them, so let my shame go where it deserves."
"To know not you as I know you?" said Love.
"For who bore the blame but I."

Then Love said, "Do you know this not?"
"For you must sit and taste the meal I have prepared for you."
So, I sat down.
And reclining with me, Love washed me clean.
Passing morsels, Love said, "Now you shall eat of this choice meal."

So I ate.
Then Love said, "Now you are Love for you have shared the meal."
And so I asked, "But what am I to do?"
And Love said, "My dear One, you shall serve."
And so I picked up the towel and began to wait upon the others.
Love saw, and smiled
Lovingly.

Love
(The Passion)

Love bade me come to walk the road of—the Via Dolorosa.
But my soul held back, for I was terrified.
I saw the Cross, which He bore, too heavy for me to bear.
Then I looked up and beheld the love in His face as He carried it,
Quick-eyed, this love pierced my heart to the wood that He held.

"Behold and behold to the Cross," Love spoke sweetly.
"For this is where I will meet and greet you."
"See this is the 'self' given for you."
And you are the body, poured out flesh and spirit.
Broken and shared, you are also lifted high, exalted.

I gazed upon the face that I saw mirrored upon the Cross.
I heard Him say, "I too am human as you."
Look and see, is not this the gaze of love?
Are we not one in our suffering?
Unexpectedly, I began to weep bitterly. Howe could I not, but weep?

Perhaps this became a part of conscious passion,
Or maybe a realization of a forgotten love, renewed.
With arms outstretched, I saw Him pass beyond the world.
With open arms, I knew I must pass now through the world.
Love invited me to walk, not weep, with the face of compassion.

Isn't this gaze necessary for the entire world to see rightly?
For the Word becoming flesh now is proclaimed "Alleluia!"
Look beyond the Cross and see the glory yet to come.
Mirror in your face the gaze of One who has walked the Way before you.
And know the power of transforming love.

Love
(The New Life)

Love bade me come…come into the water!
I was afraid, for I saw great turbulence in the churning waves.
I stayed back on the shore, in fearful resistance.
How could I survive such movement of power and sheer force?
I recognized its power to overwhelm,
Submerge and dash me about and asunder.

But, Love called forth, "Let go of your fear!
Reach out, take my hand, and let me, as Love, hold you safely."
Reluctantly, I gazed and considered my fate.
"Come! Come into the water!" persisted Love,
For I am here not for you to lose your life, but that you will find a new one."

So, I took Love's hand.
Trembling seized me,
As I let myself be led
Into submersion at Love's beckoning and embrace.
The water quickly overtook me.
Fear engulfed me.
Helpless,
The panic of ending seized me.

Suddenly, from this place of terror,
A rush of other feeling took over me
To powerful to comprehend.
I no longer feared submerging water:
The joy of Love inflamed me.

Water transformed to fire.
The fire consumed me to new life found in Love.
The water, a blazing torch of light
Penetrated my soul
Illuminated my heart.
Radiance, enlightenment,

The sacred glow shone within me.
This holy fire transformed the edges
Of all my darkness and fear:

Letting go…letting go
Letting God!
Then Love said,
"You are standing on the edge of new life.
Why wait and hold back still?
"Still?" I asked. "What more can there be?"
"Do not hold back," Love said. "Stand deeper in the water."

"Where and how do I go deeper?
Love said, "The horizon is still beyond you.
You have seen for yourself the One that is Love,
But look beyond…
Never again let go,
For the water is not around you,
But is in you, as you.
Listen carefully, so that you might hear
The voice of the One who pours the water in you.
This One is called Perfect Love,
For I am merely a reflection of the water.
And you are now in Perfect Love's fire", said Love.
Then Love departed me.

Love
(The Joy)

Love then, being quick-eyed, took me to a small hidden room,
a place simple, unadorned, filled with warmth and charm.
The window from there looked out unto the open world.
An immense view, "Un Paraiso", it was called.
I said, "My feet are upon the ground."
Love smiled, "Now, you are to be a pilgrim on a way.
Walk gently, humbly upon this ground.
The ground that you are standing on is holy, for you are holy."
Love continued, "You are to walk from this simple place.
You will return here again, after you have found joy.

Walking," said Love, "takes one into one's soul, 'the breath of joy'.
For while you have breath and feet, you are to walk.
Your life is a pilgrimage."
"A pilgrimage?" I asked. "But where am I to go?"
With a shy smile Love hesitated and then softly said,
"This pilgrimage will be long and will be tiring.
But it will bring you to a place called 'Perfect Joy',
for this is the way of the pilgrim.
You will walk among majestic mountains; pass through peaceful,
fertile green valleys, celestial highlands, stark deserts;
carved-out earthen paths will lead you down enchanting village streets;
enduring, you will withstand torrential rains, blazing sun, gripping winds
and freezing snow.
And you shall walk, and walk, and walk.
You are a pilgrim, for you are looking to observe what already resides within.
Your eyes will see; your heart will understand--beauty.
This is you!"

Then Love said, "Take only what you need, and you need only yourself.
I will provide all that you desire."
After this, Love led me to the base of a very high mountain,
sharp and pointed at the peak.
The mountain stood, seemingly insurmountable.
Beside it there was an ancient hilltop ceremonial village.
Love said, "It is my desire to give this to you; let it be your desire to find it.
Now you are to walk, climb to the very top, to the sky of heaven."

With divine assistance I began to rise and scale the mountain.
It was treacherous and perilous.
Looking down filled me with pure fright, looking up--with awe.
Love, it seemed, took me by the hand.
"Do not look back," said Love.
"You must ascend; there is no descent."
Reaching the summit—a pinnacle that pierced into heavenly realms—
I tried to grasp the beauty. It engulfed even as it eluded me.
Baffled and weary from the climb, I stood alone above the clouds.
The cloak of clouds shaded me.

Standing, looking down on the sacred village below,
I reached out with open hands, wanting to embrace the firmament—all of it—
to press it into my breast, to take it all into myself.
Then, there appeared on the plane of mid-sky a vapor dew,
as a heavenly mist or shower.
"What is this? This strain of blue and white mist rising from below,
ascending into the sky?"

It was a fresh heavenly vapor, as sanctified incense.
It asphyxiated my heart.
Then Love took my breath away and became my breath.
I gasped for air believing I was to end here,
but it was singing, singing that came out of my mouth.
Breathless, I had no ability,
but, with the breath of Joy, my singing rose as a crescendo over the clouds.
Welled up, long forgotten, ancient songs became my breath.
Trying to utter words as prayers, I could only say "I am lost in you"
as I was wrapped in the folds of Love's caress.

Suddenly, multicolored butterflies descended upon the summit.
Only then did the sky grow clearer; it was another day, again.
People walked below, talking, laughing, their children crying.
I looked around. Love had gone—left me alone.
On the ground where Love had stood, I saw a shell.
It was a pilgrim's shell.
It seemed to beckon me, "Go lightly, pilgrim, on this earth.
Make your home in joy; carry this song into the world."

My journey down the mountain with the shell seemed orderly and effortless.
I returned to the simple room that Love had given me.
For there I could look out unto the world.
Joy was there, I knew, because Love smiled as I looked out.

Larry Gosselin, OFM

The Children of Newtown, Bethlehem
A message of hope that all might be made new in a city called New Town

In the dark cold winter sky that hung as a fog of fright,
glowed a solitary star from heaven that illuminated bright.
City of Bread, Bethlehem, was a New Town in a silent night.
Out of silence came a heartfelt cry to make all things right.

A mere child myself, in darkness, I arose and saw a newborn star,
which appeared in the heavens and seemed to be both near and far.
The star led me to follow; it came over a stable very low and bare.
I saw a newborn infant, a child lying in a manger there.

This little one, a babe was so lowly and so sweet,
I felt was born and given merely for me to meet.
"Oh, dear little one," I uttered, "You came upon a midnight bright,
when darkness was shattering and we first saw heaven's radiant light."

And there among the oxen was a glow;
I saw a new life in glory that was about to grow.
The child then seemed to come to me, even one so small,
so that I might know, His birth brought peace, born for all.

Mary, his mother, gazed, and from her arms she gave Him for me to hold.
His father, Joseph, a man so brave, whispered, "Be His messenger bold."
They both said, "Tell the world that this child is born,
so that all might know this joy, and no longer mourn."

For now, in Him, you are given to have the noble right
that His light might shine through you, and all so bright.

Here in a stable so very low and bare,
it was I who was born anew there.

That a mere child might shine in Heaven as a star so bright,
and in the darkest of nights be guided to be His perfect light.

Count the number of the stars, if you can!

Go out under the night sky
Make your way into the darkness.
Then look up and see the day bright stars.
Ruminate on this illuminating power and number.
And then try to count the number of stars, if you can!
The dome of Heaven is opened
And from here a promise is made.
Be wholly in this holy place of light.
Here even the heavens seem to declare
That Promises are given as truths declared:
"You are my chosen one."
Be still; listen! Be still; listen!
My Spirit moves you to a new land.
To the mountaintop, sent, to torch a light,
To be transformed through this visited vision.
Heaven is ripped open
Earth is ripened for radiance.
Dwell not upon this mountaintop.
Go out into the world to tell the glory
That you have seen! That you are sent! Go!
And try to count the number of stars, if you can!
The night sky isn't dark; it is the world that needs light.

Through a Window of Light

Waiting upon the rise of a new day,
Dawn holds its own stillness at rest.
Given through a window of light, hope,
That peace resides in this chamber of heart.
Be still my soul, holding unto confines of trust.
There's One, who guides feet into the path of peace.
Joy sings a morning song in anticipation of coming anew.
The Light of Christ shines!
As a lamp to guide our way.
Though we might not see,
We believe in You, here,
Looking for You to shine.
For even darkness cannot
Screen our desire for sight.
For it's only in Your light
That one comes to see right.
Love is the shade that filters
This diffusion of translucency,
That rests on this table of trust.

In the Dark Room

A chair stands in the middle of a dark room.
No light or window offers a sight to see.
Resting there peacefully alone, scuffle
To find a way to know where it is I sit.
Finding the wall, I handle my way along.
Hand to wall, motion the trust moving.
Corner lends a corner. Is this a square?
Moving along finds yet another corner.
The wall ends here, opens to emptiness.
May Christ shine upon foreboding darkness.
It is in Your light that we come forward to see.

One Day

One day
Drawing to a close
Among a lifetime of such.
This day filled with mysteries
Complicated, as well as adverse.
This day stands among many as
Mysteries unfold, telling a story.
This night stands alone, yet not.
For as many have gone before
And many are yet to come.
But tonight is tonight,
In life lived as
One day.

Fat Tuesday, 2010

The wonder of the face,
Shining upon us in love.
Unsure and unshaken for what it means to see.
Our eyes have only to look upon Your majesty,
Knowing the vision of Your presence to come.

As one looks upon the Son to see the light of day,

Place in us this gift of vision,
that gives us wonder and joy.
Hold us as hope to Yourself,
for kindness and grace bid us,
"come and see."

Impregnate my heart, during this Lenten season, to trust seeking finding You in myself.
Open and revive the disciplines that teach me to place You and Your love above all else.
For it is You who stands at the protocol of majesty to meet and greet us, welcome home.

Base to Face

To be free, to stand tall,
And face the world
With all its cares,
We must build a base
From which to gaze,
Upon the loveliness
And the tragedy
Of what we hope to be.
Lord, build this foundation as strong
As a cornerstone upholding the structure
To face any uncertainty of fortune with grace.

The Fruit of Thy Womb

Born to us in the depth of life,
One comes as if in darkness to
Be light for others to see birth.
We are to be born again, again!
It's seeing in the pangs of birth
The print of the cross also born.

Oh Christ, you as a babe are the light of the world and hope of all.
You are in us as a sign of contradiction that the weak are to be strong.
You are hope to a waiting world, and peace to those who suffer sorrow.
You, Divine Master, grant us not to seek to be consoled as to console,

To be understood as to understand,
To receive love, as to show love.
For it's in the giving we receive.
It is pardoning we are pardoned,
In dying that we are born to live.
Come again, Christ of our world,
Into the brokenness of humanity.
Bind stripes that cause us discord;
Heal wounds that cause suffering,
Illuminate a flame in the darkness,
For You are born as we are born,
And You live as we're to have life.
O come, Word of God, once again
So as to be new fruit of our womb.

J E S U S !

Hallelujah

Yet,
Too soon for speaking
This word
In repentant, Lenten time.
Hallelujah!
For thankfulness spleen is
This word,
Which, when spoken,
Is a promise.
Hallelujah!
Is not this the Jesus,
that is
This word?

"Pasa por Aqui"
Transfiguration

Standing upon this peak of glory,
Among the temples of hope,
Seeing the saving grace
"Pasa por Aqui"
White light
Of radiant dawn.
Casting brilliance upward and downward,
Leading in the footprints of His steps,
Knowing glory will be revealed
From this mountain of vision.
Spoken to the beloved
"Amor Eterno".
Follow
Me.

Patient Night

Wait amid darkness
Still of night, quiet
Patient
Awaiting darkness
In the palm of the
One
That knows dearly
Immensity of love
Sees
Light guiding love
Holds the darkness
Clearly

Into the Day

The morning waits the light
So an entry to the day begins.
Hopefulness calling wisdom,
Wisdom beckoning courage,
Courage demanding faith
Becomes morning light breaking,
Into the Day.
Shall prayer of new life
Be Light?
I see the "I AM"
all in all.

Rest Assured that All is Well

Rest assured that all is well
In this love, where we do dwell,   Wellsprings here, our ringing bell,
Signaling courage, very well.   Enter then your peaceful cell.
Knowing that you and all
Are well.

Planted for Sunlight

rising light
sheds growing
in sunlight planted
rose of peace
the sweet fragrance
will blossom
this bud of hope
bloom
where
you are planted

A Lone Place Alone

Wanting to be
The person that I know to be
Not happening.
In this lone place alone
With One
Whose loves greatest
Here alone.
Come into this place alone
So I might
Be alone, Love,
In the Alone.

Planted for Peace

```
        E      R
     V            I
   O                N
 C                    G
```

beside peaceful waters
shade for rest &
peppered beauty,
sits the sacredness
Of the One.
Come to me, all in your weariness,
Who may find your life burdensome.

I refresh you;

Take my yoke

Upon you, for

My yoke's easy

And My burdens

are

Light.

White Lily
Solemnity of St. Joseph, Husband of Mary

A humble branch
grows among the lilies.
Wood for carving
The Son will crosier a cross.
A staff in hand
Leads to a pure way of faith.
Follow a dream:
This is my son and my wife.
Builds us a home
Where we will make bread.
Work of our hands
Has shown us Our Father.

I Heard the Sound of Singing

Growing among the thorns and roses
Comes the song of someone singing.
The sound so clear I hardly knew
It was there to comfort, reassure.
Your voice heard in winter-
Song calmed the night
As hearing angels
Praising hymns
Brings light
To heart.

The Fragrant Aroma of Bread

As within
deep in the soul,
is the Bread of Love.
The spirit waits to be fed.
Virgin land and sacred woods
cannot satisfy the longing to taste
the bread that takes you to distant lands
where the soul bears this trackless hunger.
What is this, this yearning to be fed by you?
How can one live without this food from Heaven?
All times to linger upon this fragrant aroma of bread
rising upward, inward, outward to taste beyond the seen.
Oh, taste and see, yes, taste and see, the goodness of the Lord,
the food that brings a new homeland, spacious, wide, and vast,
to the people that hunger for the hidden sweetness of true bread.

Raindrops
Wonderfully Made in Your Name

Raise up, oh distant mountains, deserts and wastelands,
For from you shall come one called at birth.
Youthful hopes and dawns of promise
Shine upon us in your Name.
Fragments of Holiness,
Chosen One,
For you are
To be called
John.

John.
In this your name,
Rains nourish the earth,
as if baptized anew by you.
Shrubs and herbage will sprout
springing forth with abundant life
raindrops of new life, hope, wonder.
Baptismal water generously poured forth
a new flowing life, rushing in these waters,
feeding, nurturing, bathing, washing, sending,
nourishing a seed, proclaiming, planting a hope.
Sprout to break forth, shine from the root of Jesse,
His Name is called Holy One, Counselor, Emmanuel.
God with us!
Jesus.
Rain down, Rain down, Rain down, Rain down upon us!

I Am On the Way

The phone rang,
a very impatient voice asked
"Where are you?"
I answered, "I am on the Way!"
I guess I must have sounded unconvincing,
because there was a long drawn out silence
that set in on the other side.
Really, I was headed skyward, or so it seemed,
a tireless traveler on a beam of a homespun star.
I bewildered myself, surprised by not knowing.
Where was I on this journey?
Did the knowing matter?
For example, every year, not grasping it,
I have passed the anniversary of my upcoming death,
neither knowing when, where, or how.
But I am still here, on the Way.
It sounds somewhat persuasive to be able to say,
"When I was young!"
Imagine, if all the clocks died,
no one was looking at time,
for there was nothing to measure,
"Where are you?"
Or
"Who is the greatest among you?"
If you wish to arrive first, and to be first,
You must, first, be the servant of all.
Whoever becomes like a little child
has arrived to the place where they are going.
Just then,
I received another call, different than before,
The calm caller asked, "Where are you?"
I answered again, but this time more assuredly,
"I am on the Way!"

Inspired by the Gospel of Mark 9:30-37

Ascent

journeying onward
stepping upward
onto the ledge
each crevice
holds up on
traversing
traveling
securing
moving
upward
onward
slowly
step by
step
h
e
l
d
In trust of the one who reaches for your hand.

Jug of Oil for the Widow of Zarephath

Walking the road
gathering sticks for a fire,
to cook food that would last,
for this would be the final meal,
provisions had reached the bottom.
Then in the dark of true hunger
there shone a light,
as if a candle
appeared.
Into the darkness,
in my moment of thinking,
I heard the heart of bread speak;
it emerged with demanding confidence.
"Give me your bread!" it said with assurance.
Bread of Life was asking of me for my bread.
It seemed to be saying, "Be bold, my little one,
for now you have food that you do not know."
Strong as the light, there appeared baskets
filled with bread, fruit, choice wine.
A banquet of fare to last forever.
I ate, and never again
hungered.

Based on the First Book of Kings 17:10-16

Sacred Oils

Bringing together
Oils to bind,
Bringing to work
Oils to bless,
Bringing to union
Oils to heal
Bring to birth
Oils to invite
Bringing to anoint
Oils to speak.
Sacred Oils, Sacred People
Live in Christ
Be the Chrism
In Sacred Oils.

Today

today begins
in me
this sacred
time
holy week
born
grow
for
holiness

From this Chair

in this,
an ordinary chair
hand-carved, created
with branches of nature
simply extraordinary as placed
sitting, being, having, resting
in the comfort of prayer
to pray in this place
pure in virgin
innocence
to love
to be
held
as
o
n
e

A step in Life

The ring of life
Opens as a portal.
Love creates a hunger
towards a greater vision,
making us once again new, whole.
Taking a step forward to a blessing,
Where the way goes though unknown,
there is a trust that marks the path.
Walking together,
Guided by the One,
Whose staff is sure to protect,
We follow in the love of trust,
Knowing the hand that leads
Is surely strong in gentleness.

The Proverb

"When it happens, you will be there;
Where it is spoken, you will hear it."
So the people assembled.
Jesus spoke to them
about awaking to what is really here.
He said, "When one has awakened, a person is truly free!"
Then this old man answered,
"I have been crossing the bars of shadows
and this has held up my life.
For now I have been opened."
"Thank you for waking me!"
He then led the old man
to a silent valley full of light.
It was a clear autumn day.
The light kindled as gold
like the late leaves on a cherry tree.
And they arrived at a garden,
Nightingales sang there, even in daytime.
Radiant irises knuckled among kingly daffodils.
There the old man listened to the Mission bells ringing out.
And he came back to what he thought was forgotten.
For his ears were opened to what he heard.

Reflection on Mark 7:31-37
(Jesus heals the deaf man with a speech impediment.)

"Do Whatever He Tells You"

Sometimes in dreams I see images of heaven,
not that I have ever been there, at least not yet.
But in reality, we all find ourselves now
upon this end of the road that leads there.
In these dreams I am walking and a person approaches
alongside on the road, seemingly wanting to pass by.
Suddenly the road turns brilliantly bright.
A gentle breeze passes by and I feel it like a breath:
warm and fresh. I begin walking alongside
of this wonderful stranger who says,
"When you love the world, you will hear celestial music."
We walk along in silence; it is peaceful not speaking.
The rocks seem to be shining and glittering—
We both become very quiet in this stillness.
Then, amid the calm, there comes a voice.
"Do whatever He tells you."
When I wake from the dream, the darkness of old
seems illuminated as if the lights of heaven
have become lanterns for a wedding feast.
For the bride and bridegroom have arrived
for the marriage.
Let the wedding feast begin,
and everyone is so happy to be here.
Sound the trumpet and the sweet-sounding lute,
pour the wine!
"For when you love the world,
you will hear celestial music."

Daffodils Dangle in Daylight
(The Light Bulb)

The first hint of spring came above
the chill of winter.
A cold sunny bright day
brought the first glimpse of new life.
Miniature budding daffodils leaned forward
to catch the sunbeams.
Life is indeed like that: miniature growth
groping to capture the light.
Sometimes life reminds me of being a mere child
and walking into a forest,
where there lies a hidden graceful clearing
filled with King Alfred Daffodils.
The forest is mostly dark, and somehow
the darkness wells even richer than the light
and more blessed, provided that we stay brave
and keep our sights on going in
and not holding back in fear.
It can be like the water of a river
that flows torrentially deep, but in the sunlight what
looked to be darkness was really part of the light.
The flowing water grows new life.
It was in this water that I saw
that I am seen as I believe I am.
The graceful water of baptism gently reminds
us of the glimmer of light held in the darkness,
as daffodils hidden in a forest clearing
reach for the light, holding a secret.
The secret known and told to all:
"You are my beloved One.
On you my favor rests."
Reach for the light.
Open your petals—
even in winter.
Blossom
Bloom!

What Did You Think—
That Joy Was Some Little Thing?

A newborn penguin in the snow,
awakening to life is still learning to fly.
Spreading its wings above the Antarctic snow,
new life reveals the secret of its ascent in nature.
We, also, find our souls sky-bound to a
winged life:
awakening to fly in ascent to be lifted into the
heavens.
One who encounters joy dwells in the sunrise
of eternity.
In meeting life on life's terms, and then in the
face of it all,
sprouting, spreading wings and flying, kissing
life in rising,
Gladdened by the day with promise of a new
shining world,
we are like a rose-colored candle flickering in
the darkness.
What did you think— that joy was some little
thing?
To live that which is lovely is the joyous gap.
Yes, the little penguin is learning to fly
Even in a frigid, fragile world.
And so can I.

December 15, 2012
3rd Sunday in Advent

The Pond at the Hermitage of Saint Clare

Sublime tranquility residing at this quiet pond,
Simplicity mirrored by clear water.
Beauty reflected in light.
Sister Clare,
city lights, night stars,
Brother Sun, Sister Moon,
Belonging to and longing for heavenly hosts.
Yearning, coming, drawn to this wellspring of grace,
Come to drink here from the streams of such rich delight.
Given food to eat, we know not how, to be living bread.
Finding that time waits here for you, just to be.
To be hidden alone, with all that is Alone.
To be at one, being wholly with the holy.
Calming busy minds, restless spirits,
Jesus said to the storm, "Be still!"
And then, "I am living water."
Wandering he calls us back.
Come to this pond often,
Water so as to breathe.
Jesus, Jesus, Jesus.
You, Breath of Life,
breathe upon us.
Sister Clare,
as clear water
reflects light,
mirror us
in to the
Christ.
Amen.

Christ Rises from the Dead

There is no salute of guns,
only everywhere in the world
there are those who are aware
of a silence
that is audible,
a voice
that is heard only inside
the heart,
telling the wordless secret
of ultimate joy.
Now
in the church
the priest is blessing the water.
How beautiful water is!
and selfless.
Christ has made it
miraculous
with His life
It is our birth.

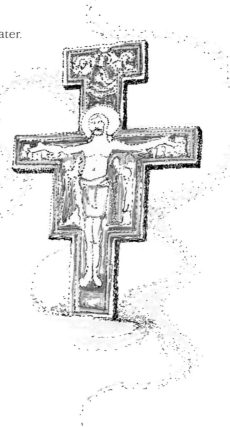

A glorious adventure set before us

O Lord!
Each day a reawakening to mystery,
Our souls magnify the Lord.
Choirs of angels sing
"Wonderful, insurmountable in wonder!"
Is Your gift to us.
May our walk today be guided in joy,
following in Your footprints,
knowing each step is a fresh encounter with Your love.
Open the skies to reveal new gifts of life.
Let it shower all in beauty and grace.
Open eyes to see, ears to hear
The joy of living in Your presence.
Walking each day, living abundantly,
in gratitude.
We stand ever mindful of your goodness,
O Lord!

Falling Awake

Mindful that mindfulness is necessary,
Two eagles fly over as I rest on the beach.
Laying aside thoughts to put on a new mind,
Holding a feeling of wonderful blessing, the ocean stillness resides within.
It can be calm and then there are storms.
All the while undercurrents are in flow.
The surface is where the drama resides,
The depth is where the mystery flows.
Sand formations creating patterns show forth the work of ebb and flow.
Two eagles look at me, and seem to wonder who I am,
I look at them and know.

Patient WabiMoon

A
Moon Rise
Gently Lifting
Full Colors Aglow,
Balanced Letting Go.
Radiant Splendor
Harmony Dwells
Peacefully
In All

The Autumn Moon rises above downtown Portland. Gathered here in the
Japanese gardens that face the city, a group of strangers sit, each one in our
own place. Alone. We are joined with one vision of anticipation in welcoming
this moon to rise over our hearts and heads. Patiently soothed in flute
music
played by roving minstrel. Enjoying the company of each other quietly and
without
knowing why; The sake and sushi helps feed our souls with delight, wonder,
amusement,
beauty, and joy.
What is Wabi, you ask?
This is Wabi.

Posted in *The Way*

Seeds of Compassion

What does compassion look like? This question was posed as Seattle welcomed His Holiness, the Fourteenth Dalai Lama, and other religious leaders to the "Seeds of Compassion" gathering in April, 2008. The focus of this five-day event was to teach and empower children and youth to live with compassion. The opportune timing of this conference corresponded with the passing of the Olympic Torch on its route to China. As political sensitivities have surfaced over Chinese polices and the sovereignty of Tibet, world attention has focused on the Dalai Lama, whose teaching embodies both compassion and humor. Humble, and with a childlike simplicity, the Dalai Lama is leader-in-exile of Tibet and a spiritual leader to Buddhists around the world. Archbishop Desmond Tutu, Sister Joan Chittister, OSB, Rabbi David Rosen, and leaders from the Sikh, Evangelical Christians, Vedanta and Islamic traditions joined the Dalai Lama in a discussion panel moderated by a Zen Buddhist Master, Roshi Joan Halifax.

The gathering represented "a holy moment" of fostering compassion on a local level. His Holiness encouraged thinking with a sense of abundance rather than scarcity and working to develop a kinder and more compassionate global community. He asked, "What is your biggest bold hope for growing compassion? What is needed to widen the circles of compassion to be unlimited, to be attuned to the present moment, to escape the prison of the limited self?" Albert Einstein once said: "It is our task to free ourselves from this prison by widening our circle of compassion to embrace all living things, creatures and the whole of creation in its beauty." The Dalai Lama went on to say that it is through one's enemies that enlightenment for compassion develops.

A young person from Africa spoke about overcoming his own hatred. He had been a member of a much-feared militia of children soldiers initiated into brutality by being forced to kill their own family members. This young man told how he had overcome hatred with compassion, and had been transformed from a ruthless killer into a person who can love again.

Seeds of Compassion participants numbered 150,000. These seeds of compassion are germinating and will grow. As the Dalai Lama reminded the gathering, "In dark times do not fight the darkness: increase the light."

There is Time; there is Still Time

There is time;
There is Still Time,
> against the advance of night.
The Convent bells herald their chime of hope,
> a reassurance,
I am here,
> I am here,
>> I am here!
Do not fear,
> for I am here.
To enter into this place, this time,
> Knowing there is time,
There is Still Time.
I have called you by name,
You are mine
I love you!
Your mind cannot comprehend this,
But your heart can respond to it.
There is time,
There is Still Time.

Rain on the Graves

Fresh soft rain on the graves of loved ones.
Gently it reminds of the quiet rest to come.
The peaceful falling
descending while
ascending,
from above
to below.

Cold Coffee on a Hot Day

A little cold coffee on a hot day and blackened with age stirs freshness in me.
Sitting by the beach, warmth of sunshine—

> Peacefulness of gentle ways of waves reading a good book
> Knowing a friend who cares
> Life being renewed with promise on the horizon—

All might not be right with the world, but it seems so now in my little humble patch of it
Letting go—sweet surrender to all that is—all that will be—
It is too little to say "Thank You", but my words are eternal and that is all that is necessary.

> The epicenter of life does revolve and evolve around bliss.
> If there is more than this I don't need to know it.

Thankfulness releases me from the cloistered living inside my head—
This is my job—to get along with myself.

> The cold coffee becomes a part of me—Awaken to all
> In gratitude.

Silent Morning

Rains passing
through streetlamps
descends as grace
translucent
transformed
hidden and bidden
showers soft of gentle light
as they stream the darkened path
illuminating the quiet glow of dawn
invigorating drops of heaven.
Awakened in vitality
with gratitude
Silent Morning
All is calm
All is bright.
A herald of hope
hides in illumination
these gentle reminders hold us
to All that which falls from above.
The morning rises with her own light
while still these reminders linger afresh—
We are "found"—caught in this shower of light.

All that is All

Blue Heron flies overhead
Barking—or whatever blue herons do as they soar past.
The day celebrates joyful sunrays that warm the souls as they touch the body.
Who of us wants to live anything but this peacefulness?
Crows stroll across wet seaweed, newly revealed in shifting tides looking for something to munch on.
Boats, planes pass by, going in opposite directions, their destinations in tack.
Land bluffs exalt while shadowing the enduring sea.
Blue Heron tenderly inspects the receding tide flats, grabbing quickly a sharp strike,
Anticipating a catch—Self forgiveness is a glacially slow process—humbling.
Gulls pass…only they know where they are going or what they are about.
Finding the way back to the current: me.
There are always layers—
How long does this take?
A lifetime.

Authentically Alive

Breathe in the darkness
Awakened to the sound of quiet.
In solitude perceived oneness abides.
The chill of a new morning, fresh rain
Calm is the moment, assurance is given.
Sincerity sits alone in harmony of self.
Letting go reveals another step in trust.
To walk this sacred truth,
"Breath of Oneness",
All is Alive.
Take All
I have
It is
Y
O
U
R
S

.

Unself-conscious Hands

I will enjoy Heaven
for I really love my barrel-making job,
connecting each board
into one round barrel.
It's actually one of my better qualities.
Not only can I make the barrels real,
They make me real.
Frugality is one of the most beautiful words in the English language.
Happiness lives in not having things
for the best things in life are not things.
If science should ever discover the center of the universe,
Many people will be disappointed
to find they are not in it.
There is still "pure innocence"
that speaks of the universal human spirit,
gentle reminders of our common humanity.
Humility is not cowardice,
but a recognition of respect
to comprehend the imperfect with genuine religious feeling.
"If you want to see, see right at once."

Love Hungers

My work is loving the world.
Is this your hunger?
Hummingbirds know how to feverishly hover
seeking the thin, delicious sweetness,
their nectar of life.
The beautifully decorated sunflowers
Draw the rapidly flying little hungry birds
To themselves,
for in their giving they receive.
Both hunger to be fed and to be food.
Love hungers.
There is a voice that cries out in hunger for mercy,
searching for living food.
So, taste and see! O, taste and see! Yes, taste and see
the goodness of the Lord,
the sweet nourishment of true food:
His body, His blood.
Living bread that comes down from heaven
To bring life to the world.

God's Mirror

I look into the sky,
The evening clouds have slipped away.
The night sky illuminates her ceiling
With dazzling lights.
Somewhere out there is a new earth
A new Heaven,
A dwelling place of eternal harmony.
Am I looking at God?
Or is this the mirror of my soul?
Both light and darkness are there.
But now. Yes, now!
I want to gaze. I want to sing. I want to be.
Pero, ya ves, estoy solo aqui!
But, you see, I am alone here!
Alone with the Alone.
Alone, but never alone.
The sky keeps inviting me
To soak, sink, stretch, and to sit
Into the heart of it all.
To reflect the above,
Yet here, within.
To see, as to be,
The moon as mirror
Rising in the dark sky
reflecting light.
Is this too much to ask or too little?
To sit at the hand of the One
Who is the light of the world.
Inside I hear…
Can you drink of the cup that I must drink?
In the darkness of the night
I was held in her utter silence.

STEVE
KALAR
©90

We Three

In silent darkness we travel,
traversing boundaries of earth and heaven,
keeping watch, staying on course through these lonesome, awesome nights.
A star bids us to follow, follow, follow!
Shadows of footprints left on the desert sand are cast by the light of a star.
We have lost ourselves to find ourselves on this poignant journey.
This ride has taken us beyond boundaries of life and death,
not knowing where we are heading.
We have left the world to come into its heart.
His light has bid us to come, "Come and see!"
How much longer will the constellations conceal Him?
When will He reveal this communion?
What we envision, what we hope to find, is the universe through Light.
In the hushed, joyous night, intimate darkness
we wait to find Him, to know Him, for we have seen His star arising.
Can anyone cross over the shore of the universal soul but this One?
This infant king whose star has shown its one light for all.
We bring you treasures, but you are the beloved treasure,
for what we seek moves our hearts to tremble;
and we are rocked through a wave of wisdom.
Your star appears in the night and then day becomes invisible,
hidden, You are manifested to all.
Your pure ray of golden light appears and gleams
for us travelers, whose whole soul is tingling on the brink of joy.
O Holy and Vigilant One, come as a fiery, expansive radiance into the world
for all to perceive your illuminating light.

A Christmas Prayer for Peace

God,
Mighty One,
Creator of all that is good,
You come to us as spirit born anew,
A child in earthen clothes and heavenly light.
Swaddling clothes you are wrapped in, for restricting movement.
You give us true freedom, as arms are opened to embrace all on a cross.
Light born in darkness, Work spoken in silence, King crowned in poverty,
Come to us again, once again, as before, as always to a world hungry.
Come, come, come to us, renew the promise of peace that is You.
Fill our void, heal our scars, calm our fears, enflame our love.
May the fear of terror and the terror of war be healed.
For Peace on Earth is still our most fervent prayer.
May guns be called to silence, anger stilled,
All nations surround by good will.
Let the dawn of your birth
Awaken us to you,
Jesus,
Christ,
Messiah,
God with us,
Prince of Peace,
Wonderful Counselor,
Root of Jesse, Star of David.

I have to wake up before dawn to see for others the first light of day

There are moments, days or even years,
when we think "I have seen this all before",
like putting on soiled clothing on a sullen day.
We have worn this garment too many days already.
But nothing is the same, for everything can be seen
with awakened eyes, to see the new light of day, again, for the first time,
Moments that come as transparencies, reminders that we are fresh anew.
Terra firma, as they call it,
rests here where we are.
There's a kindly gentleman
who lives down the street,
some kind of birth defect
made him and his daughter
blind, unable to see the light
of a new day.
At times it hurts to see them.
So I took it upon myself to
see each new day for them.
And I, feel so fresh and new,
for I am seeing in their eyes.
They are giving me new sight.
In this novel, original first light
I see the world recreated anew,
the brightened leaves of autumn,
shadowy apricots ripening in the air.
All is unfolding, unrolling, new,
I know my eyes have been opened,
I have seen the first light of day.

As Flame is to Fire

St. Augustine said,
"Our Hearts are restless until they rest in Thee."
How can our hearts not come to rest in Thee?
For we are planted in the seed of contemplation
Sealed in the dark and waiting to be born.
Night is our home and silence is our life.
Poverty is our wealth and helplessness is our security.
We are exiles in the far end of solitude
And there we are living as listeners.
We are awakening to receive the Christ of our night
For He is the Lord of the day.
Joy is our vocation.
Ecstasy is our mission.
We are burning with joy.
We need no eloquence here
For we are tongue-tied to express what we cannot fully comprehend.
To receive this Christ is as white is to lightening.
And flame is to fire,
The wind is to sky.
Come quick desired One
For we have been resigned too long in expectation.
As we sing now in this stone valley of hope,
here you are on the breath of dawn.
Let your light shine for all to see,
this dawn of a new day.

Las Palomas de Mexico

Mi gusto sentarse en un banco del Mision y alimentar a las palomas.
(I like to sit on the bench of the Mission and feed the doves.)

This old, sacred church of Santa Anita, Jalisco, Mexico,
as a humble temple, enlivening a humble people of prayer,
magnificently towering above, with simple, shining, splendor…
Herein rises a royalty with an antiquity, as Mother and Queen.
Doves of this Franciscan Convent rest in the inner sacred garden,
knowing the sound and serenity of Mission bells, they come and go,
at one will soaring and returning in flight, filling the sky in procession.

I love to sit
here, now, among the beautifying roses of this sacred garden,
remembering a time past, traveling into the rugged mountains,
looking for another sacred place and finding it among the poor.
To think, "He who has made us, of nothing, has called us to life."
Loving, I would like to remain and be planted firmly as these roses,
in this garden sacred, and free as doves of the Mission are able to fly.

Grand Parents

Can you recall grandparents who were strong?
from following a plow in order to touch the earth with their hands and soul.
Grandparents held memories to be told,
stories that seemed to smell of onions, soap, and wet clay,
as did they.
They seemed to make us want to be strong and sturdy.
Or remember the winter mornings, when we awoke to the sound of
crackling fire,
and the warmth of the hearth that held back the cold.
The hearth was the heart,
as the heart is a hearth.
We can all be strong, sturdy, warm, and glowing,
like singing birds
securely nestled in a strong, green oak branch.
We can be like an old apple tree
whose boughs are bent over, producing the thickest fruit.
The human heart is the family,
and family is the human heart.
Both pulsate with the rhythms of love.
We all know "Life is not any crystal staircase."
It has tacks in it, and splinters as well.
But, somehow those memories that we carry
see us through.
Once in a while, we need to summon out the past,
the gift of the person we are, even before we came into this world.
We have come to know divine love with human hands and hearts,
for all we are and all we have, we are first given a family.

Eye See, I Say and Be Sent!

I was born blind,

And there is one thing I know
for sure, at this point in my life:
I am not going to die young.

But now, I say, my eyes can see.
I don't think of it as eyesight deficit,
but as foresight profit.

I see things I have never seen before:
the beauty that is too far
beyond human sight.

The blindness of the past is gone.

It is as if my eyes have been trained
to see through a window with no color.

To stand at this open window and gaze
and see the light of one candle.

A light in a new world, as if it is,
The Light of the World.

It was this man, I do not know who,
but he opened my eyes.
And now I see, and stand in light that shines.

For many years, it had been night.
Now in the day, I piece together a life
that has a journey beyond this world.

In this new world, with light and sight,
A distant glimmer motes in my eye,
Leads me into a cool hour, under the bridge of light.
I recognize the unrecognizable One.

A Prayer for Mother Teresa
For the Feast of St. Therese, the Little Flower

O Most Loving Father,

In the feast of October, we turn our hearts to remember, with the greatest of devotion and love, the purest blossom and fragrance of beauty and simplicity, that You have bestowed, in our Little Flower of Your Son Jesus, Saint Therese.

In her life and love for You, a little rose has been planted in the sweet garden of our souls, and in this garden, we learn to know the simplicity of Your love. In this childlike trust, we, again, place ourselves into Your most loving hands.

And as a young bird, that is unable to take flight, we also let our fledgling wings rest in the subdued presence of Your peace and love. For, with You, there is nothing to fear.

Now, in the season of Autumn, we await upon the hope of Spring, to release forth new life. Our hearts are ready, O God. Our hearts are ready.

With Therese, we look towards the dawn, to shine forth the radiance of new light, and in the shadow of early morning, our hope is stirred. May this new life be for us a light, a light that will dispel the darkness of ignorance, pride, and selfishness.

But if there be darkness, O God, let it only be as You would have chosen to will it. For it is only Your light that enlightens. We ask that the splendor of Your countenance will be in our hearts as a light that never fades.

O Most Precious Lord, Jesus,

On this day, we once again give to you our hearts, which are filled with the greatest thanks and praise, for another most precious and beautiful little flower, that You have caused to bloom among the poorest of the poor.

This Teresa, is also a little flower of Your great beauty and peace, because she shines forth the radiance and the magnitude of your satiated thirst for us. And in the fragrance of this Little Flower of Calcutta, flows Your gift of compassion and charity, that reveals to us Your most loving and merciful face.

As a tender shoot, that has been planted and watered in the vineyard of your Kingdom, to the poorest of the poor, may this Little Flower, Teresa, be for you also a gift of Your thirst, that You have so humbly offered to us, in our dearest Mother Teresa and where You have revealed your disguised face with such great love for the poorest of the poor.

So, today we join our voices and hearts with all the Heavenly voices, in giving You praise and thanks, for Your dear Little Flower, St. Therese, and for the example of purity and love that she has shown to us. And in our hearts, thus filled with this love for You, we are also filled with joy in our thirst to become a more pure example of Your most tender love and charity.

O Most Loving, Love,
Bless our dearest Mother Teresa on this day of joy and praise. May her heart and soul be only You and may she become more and more like the purest of all souls given to You. May the glory of the radiance of Your Most Holy Spirit shine forth upon her. May You, Lord Jesus, continue to live in her life, to look through her eyes, to walk in her steps, and to love with her heart. And let all be only for You. And, when we look up from where we are, may we not see her but may we only see Your face, O Lord.

Dearest Mother Mary,

Look down with Your Motherly Love on Your dearest servant, Teresa, in her love for You. Now may You be the cause of her joy, protect her in weakness and strengthen her in faith. Throw Your mantle of purity over her and present her to Your Divine Son as a pure vessel of Your love.

Heavenly Father,

I Ask All Of This In The Name Of Jesus Our Lord.

Feast of St. Therese of the Little Flower
October 1, 1995
Mother House of Missionaries of Charity, Calcutta, India
In celebration of the Feast Day of Mother Teresa given the name
"The Little Flower of Calcutta"

A little field sun bee

There is a blessing walking on the open road,
as the grace of a woman on a journey
with her pilgrimage of life.
El Camino Real
del Rey.

At the beginning of time and the light of day,
the birds unfurl a joyous song:
you are never alone.
El Camino Real
del Rey.

For there is another walking along side,
as the air, not there,
He is your brother.
El Camino Real
del Rey.

There is a line that all must cross one day
that separates life and new life,
where all are singing,
El Camino Real
del Rey.

Notice moving through the little field of life
the sun bee gathering sweetness,
then all will be honey.
El Camino Real
del Rey.

The above poem was inspired by E. Littlefield Sundby
(pronounced "Sun Bee"), a woman on a pilgrimage on
El Camino Real del Rey, ("The Royal Highway of the King")
Californian Mission Trail

Pike Place

The landlubber tourists wade through the wet, crowded, open-aired, legendary market,
   lined with an artful array of visual displays—the best of nature and talent—
colorful, local flowers, works of art, leather crafts, multicolored fresh fruits, and vegetables,
   and fish.
Yes, an array of life as food from the sea.
This place feeds your senses.
Fish: the very heart of the Public Market and Seattle.
People come from near and far, across the globe, just to see this soulful Piscean exhibit.
And the world-famous fishmongers, their orange waders and rubber boots,
   hearties at shouting out:
   commanding, compelling, joy and enthusiasm,
   entertaining and magnetizing the curious crowd of onlookers.
These earthy anglers are the heart of the city, renowned for its rain, coffee and fish.
Notorious and noble salesmen—but hardly saints.
The characters bellow out while crowds gather round,
     "Watch out! Fish do fly!"
Then, unexpectedly, a huge red snapper sails through the audience,
   and is faithfully caught near a startled onlooker's cheek.
The crowd cheers, begging to see more "flying fish".
"Watch your head; you might be struck!"
Watch your wallet; you might be tempted to buy a flying fish.
I've landed here, myself being a fisher.

My purpose as fishmonger is to animate the masses, make people happy, excited, eager.

I know how to work the crowd. I am 'front and center', good at what I do.

People ask me, "Have you always been a fishmonger?"

  "No," I answer. "I done other things."

Then comes their question (as an answer), "Are you a priest?" as if they already knew.

"Yes," I say. "I'm a Franciscan Priest."

"So, what are you doing being a fishmonger? How did you end up here?"

"Well," I say, "Jesus told his followers that following him might be more than pretty fishy.

You know, He called His first followers as fishermen to leave their boats and nets

    and become fishers of men and women—so, here I am!"

"I guess Jesus' call means that your hands are going to end up caked with fish scales,

    in a public way, and you'll be coming home smelling and looking really 'fishy'."

"Isn't that what it means to be a fisherman?"

"So let me ask you, do you really believe that fish can fly?"

"Well, let me tell you, I have tagged each one of these salmon with a prayer.

If they land near you, you are caught, and you are part of the daily catch.

And I have never let a salmon drop yet, and I don't plan to.

So, you're not off the hook until you set your life flying like those fish.

Let me put it another way. Do you believe *you* can fly?

Well, you can!" I say. "You've got wings, you know, like an angel.

So then, will you buy this salmon and take it home?

We can pack to ship anyway.

By the way, do you love Jesus? Would you want to follow Him?

How to be a Poet

write
dream
whisper
imagine
imagine
whisper
dream
write

Love, laugh, live, grow, smell, hear, see, feel,
teach, travel, wander, question, explore, amuse.
Open your soul to all that is good, beautiful and holy.
Articulate love: inspire another: plot new magic: entertain mystery: excite
people:
illustrate life: enter spirit: take stock: tome a story: desire character: fill
empty time:
turn away fear: give description to a hero: stay in the middle: have an
ancient voice:
crack beneath language: begin asking, why?: tell about underwater sea
monsters:
never fight back: open your will: judge from above: believe in, "only if" and
"what if":
have no villains: show good faith: curl the pages of life: give words to life, life
to words.

Get up early in the morning to pray and write, then write and pray.
Have the heart and wonder of a child, and the soul and passion of a mystic.

Here! Hear!

Who do you say that, I Am?"
When God's voice seems silent,
Where is God when life is rough?
Here! There!
Hear! Listen!
Lord, is there a verb we speak for "You"?
For You are moving in and out of our lives.
Like a breath that leaves the sentences open.
Unanswered, but heard.
Who am I?
Who are you?
The great question of St. Francis of Assisi.
Peter is asked, "Who do you say that I am?"
For You come whispering with a new language,
From words unspoken, that have not yet occurred.
Take us to Your side of silence,
Take us with You as Your own.
For on Your side of silence, here, we listen, we hear.
May the distance not elude the sound of Your breath.
Knowing that we long for another language,
And here we strive to hear its meaning.

Beginnings

Beginning today,
    beginning the day.
Beginning to pray,
    this is the beginning.
Lord, may today be as a new beginning.
May each day begin with this beginning.

In Memoriam
Brother Kelly Cullen, OFM
September 10, 1953 to November 13, 2010
A poem written by him, *Given Today*

GIVEN TODAY

I WAS GIVEN A ROCK TODAY
FROM AN OLD AND VERY DEAR FRIEND,
A BROTHER TO MY SOUL.
AND IT WAS A MOST SPECIAL ROCK
WITH A SIMPLY POWERFUL MESSAGE:
HELLO. I LOVE YOU.
GOOD MORNING.

NATURE TELLS THE TRUTH.
MY FRIEND AND I,
BOTH FROM THE STATE OF WASHINGTON,
HAVE KNOWN EACH OTHER
AND HOW NATURE SPEAKS TO US
FOR YEARS.

SO THE SHARING OF AN OCEAN-POLISHED ROCK,
CUDDLED AND CARVED WITH SUCH PONDEROUS AFFECTION
BY SCORES OF SEASONAL STORMS
AND EVEN MORE SUMMERS
HOLDS MEANING,
A MESSAGE BEYOND APPEARANCES,
A MEETING OF OUR HEARTS.

AND THIS IS MORE TRUE NOW,
HAVING WATCHED THE FILM "DEPARTURES",
A JAPANESE FILM ABOUT REVERENCE,
REVERENCE FOR DEATH—AND LIFE—
AND HOW WE TELL EACH OTHER
I AM GLAD YOU ARE THERE,
GRATEFUL YOUR LIFE LIVED
CLOSE WITH MINE.

I WAS GIVEN A ROCK TODAY.
A HELLO. AND I LOVE YOU;
I AM SO VERY GLAD YOU ARE HERE.

Ignatian Prayer

Nothing is more practical than
Finding God, that is, than
Falling in Love
In a quite absolute, final way.
What you are in love with,
What seizes your imagination,
It will decide,
What will get you out of bed
In the morning,
What you do with your evenings,
How you spend your weekends,
What you read, who you know,
What breaks your heart,
And what amazes you with
Joy and gratitude.
Fall in love, stay in love,
And it will decide everything.

–Attributed to Pedro Arrupe, S.J.
General Superior of the Society of Jesus,
1965-1983

Prepare the Place

He needs a place.
We need a place to lay him.
Let us place him here in the cave.
He can rest in this carved out place in rest.

He came to this place.
This place of death and sorrow.
He prayed for him in the place of death,
In this place He raised him up beyond this place.

Lazarus, come out of this place,
For I come to this place that is not death.
Come out of this place! Come out of this place.
For there is a place past death--to the place of new life.

And so He prayed and taught us,
to pass from this place to the new place.
Come to this place! Come to this place! All of you!
Roll back the stone! Break forth the vault! Open the grave!

Prepare for yourself this place of rest.
Here you lay, not in death but in eternal life
Come to this place! Come to this place! All of you!
Remove the burial linens, untie yourself, and may you be free!

For you are free here in this place,
Free to live, to move, and to have your being.
Come anew to this place! Come to this place! Come anew!
Let the stench of death be removed with the fresh fragrance of life.

Ghosts of Celilo Falls

Submerged
in back waters
lies the living spirit
of a people.
Stories
of old
told on these river banks,
swift waters that could carry you
away, of strong currents cascading over rocky
crags and salmon beneath those make-shift fishing jetties.
For a river has been changed, a time has past. It lives on but as a memory
beneath deep waters now. Flow on...river...flow on past the rails and bridges that can carry
us calling to another distant shore where songs are sung. Give strength to walk
planks that helped us cross–nets cast in rushing waters, welcoming a yell,
"Fish on!" For once salmon swam, waiting to be caught. Alas,
no longer do they cry "Look for me..."
We swim deep and so must
you
y
o
u
!

Editor's note: Celilo Falls was the traditional fishing site for the indigenous people who lived along the Columbia River. This sacred place was submerged with the backwater created by the Bonneville Dam on the Columbia in 1937. The Native People of this area believe that "someday" this sacred place will re-emerge, as it now lies hidden below these waters of the river. The image of an eagle or osprey in flight symbolizes the spirit of these fishermen.

Habemus, Papa Francisco

Out on the balcony, he walked
bewildered and afraid,
people in expectant darkness,
held sparkling lights
hands and hearts, illuminating
the Roman night sky.

The Latin American People
glowed with joy,
for our Latin Holy Father.
We have a Francis.
"To rebuild my little church"
spoke the Roman sky.

Holy Father,
thus we call you,
"Francis, the Humble."
As Francis, the Poverello,
Our Seraphic, Holy Father.
Bless, our humble brother,
O Father, make him holy,
as You art in Heaven.
Who art, All Good,
Glorious God,
Most High.
Amen.

Out on the balcony, he bowed,
gentle and strong,
people in love and gratitude,
held him in prayer
heads bowed in humbleness
in the Roman night sky.

Delight
to Be light

For the wonders of day
awakens at dawn a ray,
to come to light to pray.

Come to this day, that is,
may birth of joy, to stay,
the mind, so not to fray.

Lord, of Light, be here,
in Your coming of light
to be all this is Delight.

Enlight

It's in your light
That we see light.

Open the eyes of our heart to see
rightly and brightly rays of light.

Be still, still be,
night's stillness.

For in Your light is the stillness
That is still yet to come to dark.

Enlighten eyes,
To wait in dark.

Into Heaven

There is a place we enter into,
  sometimes quite unknowingly,
that transcends us,
  like seeing a lifting cloudbank
  rising above coastal mountains,
unveiling portals in the sky,
  as if knowing love for the first time.
Shuddering in joy, we see Heaven suddenly opened–
  a portal understanding, insight given,
linking Heaven to Earth,
  Earth to Heaven.
Wonders open our eyes seeing
  what lies beyond, and yet here.
The hill of crucifixion and the garden of resurrection
  so fittingly placed near each other.

A voice says, "Are you looking for Me?"

  "Yes, I am! I long to see You."

"I am here, in the garden."

  "Where are You hidden?"

"I'm here, calling out your name...for you."

  "Let me see. Let me see...for I want to see" I plead.

"When you really look for Me, you will see Me instantly,
for it is Mine to give you, this vision of what lies hidden.
  What I give you now is my joy, as yours for all time.
Live in this joy, for you are in Me.
  I am in you, with you...always.
Together we live."

And, to you, dear Reader

Circle of Light

The sunflower, lovingly smiled
in the warmth of the sun,
turned its sun–drenched face,
into the light,
saying,
Thank you,
for being,
Light.

Mirror, Pure Light

"Look at your face reflected in His and let your heart
    sing.
What marvelous humility.
What astonishing Poverty.
The king of the angels, the Lord of life, a child should
    be.

Make yourself beautiful daughter of God and spouse of
    the King.
Look at your face reflected in His, and let your heart
    sing.
So run and do not delay.
His sweetness lightens the way.
His kiss is the happiest kiss of all,
And love is your life.

And cover yourself with the flowers, and cover yourself
    with the robe,
And cover yourself with the glorious life
Of Christ your Lord.
Of Christ your Lord."

–St. Clare of Assisi

About the Author

Fr. Larry Gosselin, OFM is a Franciscan Friar of the Province of Saint Barbara. Fr. Larry was born in Sumner, Washington and is presently serving in the parish of St. Barbara at Old Mission Santa Barbara in Santa Barbara, California. Fr. Larry has served in various ministries, which include: advocacy for the homeless in Seattle, Washington; ministry among the Native Peoples of the Mescalero Apaches (N.M.), Jemez Pueblo (N.M.) and the Yakima Nation (WA.), parish ministry in Portland, Oregon and Huntington Beach, California, as well as serving as Pastor and Guardian at Old Mission San Miguel, San Miguel, California. He has lived in Guadalajara and has a special love for the Hichole People and the people of Mexico, as well as residing in other places where he has spent time: India, Bolivia, and Europe. He has a deep passion and love for poetry and a loving appreciation for the beauty of the inspired word.